CONTENTS

To the Gurus

A NOTE FROM IRA

Welcome to *Om the Yoga Dog*. I am so pleased to introduce
Om and his friends to you.

In this day of mobile phones, iPads and distractions galore,
yoga is more necessary than ever before, especially for
children because habits learnt early on remain with us for
a lifetime. In this book we focus on asanas (the postures and
movements we perform), but the benefits of yoga transcend
the physical. The ultimate benefits of the practice are the
concentration, focus and willpower that a young yogi develops.

Through Om and his friends, I have relayed my learnings at
the Sivananda Ashram where we follow ancient teachings
from the Vedas taught to us by Master Swami Sivananda and
Swami Vishnudevananda. If it wasn't for them and their
blessings, this book could never have been written.

Om Shanti.

INTRO BY OM

Namaste! My name is Om and I'm a
yoga dog. Welcome to my yoga book! Yoga
makes you strong, it makes you focused and it
gives you unlimited energy to have unlimited
fun. I've been doing yoga since I was a little
puppy and in this book I will show you all my
favourite 'asanas', or poses. Thank you for your
time and I hope you enjoy using the book and
doing yoga as much as I enjoyed writing it.

HOW TO USE THIS BOOK

The book is divided into four parts

01 WARM UP WITH OM

02 ASANAS (The Postures)
by Om, the yoga dog

03 PRANAYAMA (Breathing Exercises)
by Prana, the frog

04 MINDFULNESS
by Moksha, the elephant

We suggest that you (and your grown-up) read each part individually and then refer to the plans at the end of the book to choose which class is best for you.

WARM UP WITH OM

SUN SALUTATION

Before we start the practice of yoga,
it is important to warm up
the body in the correct way.

EVERY MOVEMENT IN YOGA MUST BE COORDINATED WITH THE BREATH. WE MUST USE THE BREATH TO CENTRE THE BODY AND TO DEVELOP FOCUS.

SUN SALUTATIONS (OR 'SURYA NAMASKARS') ARE TECHNICALLY NOT ASANAS, BUT WARM—UP EXERCISES THAT PREPARE OUR BODY FOR THE ASANA PRACTICE.

Each sun salutation consists of 12 steps
and while this may seem complicated in the
beginning and you may get everything
mixed up and twisted, keep at it and I
promise that you'll be able to do everything
perfectly very soon.

The 12 Steps of a Sun Salutation

Stand with your spine straight and arms relaxed by your side.
Inhale deeply and begin.

1 *Exhale*
Bring your palms together in prayer position.

2 *Inhale*
Stretch your arms back over your head. Keep your knees and elbows straight. Arch your hips forward.

3 *Exhale*
Bend forward, bringing your hands or fingers to the floor. Make sure your fingers and toes are in a straight line.

4 *Inhale*
Stretch your right leg back. Drop the right knee to the ground. Stretch up and back.

5 *Hold your breath*
Bring the left leg back.
Bring your body in a
straight line as if you are
doing a push up.

6 *Exhale*
Drop your knees to the
ground. Keep the hips
up and bring the knees,
chest and chin to the
ground.

7 *Inhale*
Slide up like a cobra.
Arch your chest
up and bring the
head back.

8 *Exhale*
Tuck your toes
underneath your body
and, without moving
your hands or feet,
bring the hips up. Push
the heels towards the
floor. You are now in an
upside down V.

9 *Inhale*
Bring your right foot forward between the hands in line with your fingers and toes. Drop your left knee to the ground and stretch up.

10 *Exhale*
Bring your left foot forward, next to the right foot. Bring your forehead towards the knees. Fingers and toes are in a straight line.

11 *Inhale*
Stand up. Stretch your arms up and back.

12 *Exhale*
Bring your arms forward and down. Repeat with the other leg.

SINGLE LEG RAISES

Lie down with your back on the mat, arms by your side.

1 *Inhale*
Raise your right leg up, keeping the knees straight.

2 *Exhale*
Bring your right leg down.

3 *Inhale*
Raise your left leg. Make sure your right knee is flat on the ground.

4 *Exhale*
Bring your left leg down.

Repeat the exercise three times with each leg. Do this as slowly as possible!
The slower you do this, the better.

KNEES TO CHIN

Lie down with your back on the mat and arms by your side.
Lift your head a few inches off the ground.

1 *Inhale*
Bring your right knee
to your chin. Keep
the left leg flat on
the ground.

2 *Exhale*
Lower the right leg
back on the mat.

3 *Inhale*
Repeat the same
steps with the
left leg.

4 *Exhale*
Bring the left leg
down.

Repeat this three times with each leg,
coordinating your breath with every movement.

CYCLING

Lie down with your back on the mat, arms by your side.
Raise both legs off the mat and imagine that you are cycling.
Breathe steadily, inhaling and exhaling.

Continue this for a minute. Now reverse
the direction of cycling.

Now that you're all warmed up, let's start with our asana practice.

ASANAS
(THE POSTURES)

SHOULDER STAND

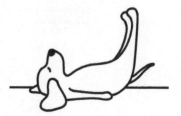

1 Lie down with your back on the mat. Bring the feet together.

2 Inhale as you raise both legs up until they are at a right angle to your body. Make sure the head and neck are on the ground.

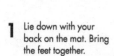

IN SANSKRIT, THE SHOULDER STAND IS CALLED 'SARVANGA' MEANING 'ALL PARTS' BECAUSE IT IS SO GOOD FOR EVERY PART OF OUR BODY!

3 Bring your hands to the hips and gently push the body up. Walk your hands down your back till you are resting on your shoulders.

4 As you hold this asana, focus on the throat.

NEVER COMPARE YOURSELF WITH OTHERS AND APPRECIATE WHAT YOU CAN DO WELL. EVEN IF YOU CAN'T DO A SHOULDER STAND, YOU MAY STILL BE ABLE TO DO A PERFECT HEADSTAND!

Never jump into this position.

PLOUGH

1 From the shoulder stand, lower both your feet towards the ground behind the head. Keep the knees as straight as possible.

2 If your toes reach the ground, bring the hands to the floor, keeping the palms on the ground. If your toes do not reach the ground, continue supporting your back with your hands.

Don't let your knees bend.

3 Hold this position for 10 seconds initially. Slowly increase the time to 30 seconds.

4 To come out of the asana, bring yourself back to the shoulder stand. Then slowly and with control lower your feet to the ground.

TIP: You can relax in-between asanas or catch your breath by lying flat on your back with your hands and legs apart (savasana).

BRIDGE

1 Lie down with your back on the mat. Bring your arms to your side.

2 Bend your knees and bring your heels close to the hips. Your feet should be hip-width apart.

3 Slowly raise your stomach, supporting your lower back with your hands.

4 Hold this position for a few seconds and breathe. Gently come down.

WHEEL

1 Lie down with your back on the mat. Bring your hands to your side.

2 Bend your knees and bring your heels close to the hips. The heels should be about hip-width apart.

3 Raise your hands and bring them back next to the ears. The palms should be on the floor with the fingers pointing towards the shoulders.

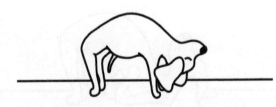

4 Lift your body up with the support of your hands and feet.

5 Maintain this position for a few seconds. Slowly lower your body till it touches the ground. Straighten your legs and arms.

FISH

1 Lie down with your back on the mat. Bring your legs and feet together. Tuck your hands under your body.

2 Bend your elbows and push them into the ground. Putting the weight on your elbows, lift the chest up.

3 Drop the head back so that the crown of your head is on the ground and the chest is expanded. Even though your head is on the floor, there is no weight on the head, only on the elbows.

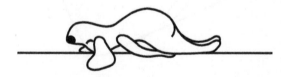

4 Stay in this position for a few seconds, breathing deeply. (Imagine you are a fish swimming in the ocean!)

5 Slowly release your head and arms and come down.

DON'T WORRY IF YOU CAN'T DO SOMETHING. YOGA CAN BE CHALLENGING SOMETIMES. THE TRUE ESSENCE OF YOGA IS SADHANA (PRACTICE) AND STIRA (PATIENCE) WHICH WILL ULTIMATELY LEAD YOU TO YOUR RESULT.

TIP: After you finish the asana, shake your head from side to side, shake your arms and your legs, releasing any tension.

BUTTERFLY

1 Sit with your legs straight out in front of you. Bend your knees and pull your heels towards your pelvis.

2 Drop your knees out to the side and press the soles of your feet together, bringing your heels as close to the pelvis as you can.

3 Hold your toes. Inhale and exhale with control. Flap your knees up and down like a butterfly's wings.

TUMMY SANDWICH

1 Sit up straight on the mat. Keep your legs together and stretch them out straight in front of you.

2 Inhale. Stretch your arms up over the head.

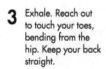

3 Exhale. Reach out to touch your toes, bending from the hip. Keep your back straight.

4 Stay in this posture. Continue to inhale and exhale comfortably.

COBRA

1 Lie down on your tummy. Touch your forehead to the ground. Place your palms flat on the floor, directly beneath the shoulders. Make sure your fingertips are in line with your shoulders and elbows are pointing upwards.

2 Inhale. Slide up like a cobra, pushing your palms into the floor. Raise your head, chest and chin, arching the back.

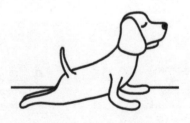

3 Keep your hips and legs on the ground and look up to the sky.

4 Stay in this position. Inhale and exhale, keeping your arms and back strong.

5 Exhale. Slowly bring your head and arms down.

6 Repeat the asana three times with controlled breathing.

BOW

1 Lie down on your tummy with arms by your side.

2 Bend the knees, separating them slightly. Take your arms behind your back. Hold both your ankles with both hands.

3 Inhale. Lift your head, chest and thighs off the ground, arching the body as much as possible.

TIP: You can rock up and down for an extra stretch!

CAT AND COW

1 Kneel on your hands and knees in a 'tabletop' position. Make sure that your knees are directly below your hips, and your wrists, elbows and shoulders are in line and perpendicular to the floor.

2 Exhale. Push your spine up, towards the ceiling. Drop your head down towards the floor. This is the cat pose.

3 Inhale. Come back to the tabletop position and exhale.

4 Inhale. Push your tail bone and chest towards the ceiling. Allow your belly to sink towards the floor. This is the cow pose.

5 Exhale. Come back to the tabletop position.

6 Repeat this asana 5 to 10 times.

ROARING LION

1 Sit with your hips on your heels. Rest your palms on your knees, spreading your fingers like the claws of a lion.

2 Inhale. Bring the chin up. Stretch your spine.

3 Exhale. Place your palms on your thighs. Arch your spine and stick out your tongue. ROAR like a lion.

4 Inhale. Come back to the starting position and repeat.

CAMEL

1 Sit up on your knees. Knees should be slightly apart.

2 Bend backwards. Grab the left ankle with your left hand and the right ankle with your right hand.

3 Inhale. Arch the back, tilting the head as far back as possible.

RELAX, RELAX AND RELAX . . .

4 Exhale. Release your arms.

5 Repeat the asana three times.

LOTUS

Om's favourite posture.

1 Sit with your legs stretched out in front of you.

2 Bend the right knee. Bring the right ankle on top of the left thigh.

3 Bend the left knee. Bring the left ankle on top of the right thigh.

4 Straighten your back. Close your eyes and hold this posture, breathing comfortably.

WARRIOR

1 Stand up with your feet three to four feet apart. Raise your arms perpendicular to the floor and parallel to each other.

2 Step forward and bend your right knee parallel to the ground. Keep your left leg straight.

3 Reach up to the sky with your arms. Arch your back.

4 Bring your arms in line with your shoulders and parallel to the ground.

5 Switch your legs and repeat the same on the other side.

TIP: Choose three qualities that you think
are important for a warrior and think of
those qualities as you try the variations.

STANDING TUMMY SANDWICH

DON'T WORRY
IF YOU CAN'T TOUCH YOUR
TOES. IN THE BEGINNING,
NEITHER COULD I!

1 Stand with your spine straight. Inhale deeply. Raise your arms up.

2 Exhale. Bend down till your fingers touch your toes and your nose touches your knees.

3 Stay in this position for a few seconds, breathing comfortably. Repeat with controlled breath.

DANCER

1 Standing up on your mat, bend your right leg at the knee. Grab your big toe and pull it towards the head.

2 Stay in this position for a few seconds, fixing your gaze on a point in front of you to maintain balance. Focus on controlled breathing to steady the posture.

3 Repeat on the other side.

TRIANGLE

1 Standing up on your mat, keep your legs two to three feet apart.

2 Bring your arms up in line with your shoulders, palms facing down.

3 Bend to the right side and touch the right toes with the right hand.

4 Stay in this position for a few seconds, controlling your breathing. Return to the standing position.

5 Repeat the same on the left side.

TREE

1 Standing up on your mat, bring your right foot to your left thigh. Rest the sole of your right foot on the inside of your left thigh.

2 Bring your hands together in a prayer position. Fix your gaze on a point in front of you to maintain balance. Focus on controlled breathing to steady the posture.

3 Bring your arms and leg down. Switch to the other side. Rest the sole of your left foot on the inside of the right thigh.

SAVASANA

or Corpse Pose

1 Lie down on the mat. Keep your arms and legs apart and your palms open and facing up. Relax.

2 Close your eyes and breathe gently and slowly. Imagine that your breath is flowing through your body like a stream.

3 Stay like this for a few minutes. Relax each and every part of your body.

PRANAYAMA
(BREATHING EXERCISES)

PRANAYAMA WITH PRANA

Pranam! My name is Prana the frog and I'm here to teach you the wonderful benefits of 'pranayama', or breathing exercises. To breathe means to live and to live means to breathe, that is why breathing correctly is so important. People always ask me how I have so much energy to hop so high and so far. It's because of pranayama and I'm happy to share my learnings with you.

BALLOON BREATHING

1 Sit in a comfortable position with your spine straight. Place your hands on your knees. Breathe in and out comfortably through your nose. Close your eyes.

2 Imagine that your body is a balloon and you are filling it with air. Arch your back, expand your chest and bring your arms over your head.

3 Exhale. Bring your arms back down and collapse your chest. Pull your tummy in and give yourself a hug.

4 Repeat for a few rounds — expanding your body as you inhale — becoming big like a balloon and then exhaling and deflating the balloon.

TRY THIS FIRST
THING IN THE MORNING
TO WAKE YOURSELF UP
AND TO HAVE A
SUPER-ENERGISED DAY.

'PRANA' IS THE LIFE
FORCE WITHIN ALL OF US.
'YAMA' MEANS CONTROL.
BY PRACTISING PRANAYAMA, WE
CONTROL THE LIFE FORCE
IN OUR BODY.

HEART AND BELLY BREATH

1 Sit in a comfortable position with your spine straight. Place one hand on your tummy and the other on your chest. Close your eyes. Notice how your breath is moving in and out of your body.

2 Inhale and exhale, paying attention to your breath. Inhale and feel your tummy become bigger as you fill it with your breath. As you exhale pull your belly button in, pushing all the air out.

3 Breathe like this, focusing on your breath, breathing slowly and comfortably.

DO YOU KNOW FROGS CAN BREATHE THROUGH THEIR SKIN TOO?

4 Breathe deeply. Imagine that you are breathing into your heart. Fill your tummy with air. Breathe a little bit more, bringing the breath to your chest.

5 Exhale. Squeeze the air out of your heart and then your tummy.

6 Continue this breathing – filling your tummy with air – then your heart and then exhaling from your heart and your tummy.

RETENTION

1 Sit in a comfortable position. Place your hands on your knees or lap.

2 Close your eyes. Breathe, focusing on each inhalation and exhalation.

3 Inhale deeply, filling your lungs with air. Hold your breath for a few seconds.

BREATH RETENTION IS A GREAT WAY TO FOCUS YOUR MIND!

4 Focus on the point in-between your eyebrows as you hold your breath. Imagine it shining like a diamond.

5 Exhale slowly. Take a few normal breaths.

6 Hold your breath again; increase the time of retention by a few seconds each time.

ANULOM VILOM

or Alternate Nostril Breathing

1 Sit in a comfortable position with your spine straight. Close your eyes and take a few deep breaths.

2 Bring your right hand to your nose, keeping the left hand on your knee. The fingers of your right hand should be in the 'vishnu mudra'.

3 Close your left nostril with your ring finger and breathe in through your right nostril.

Vishnu Mudra: The index finger and middle finger are curled into the palm and the other three fingers are resting on your nostril.

4 Close your right nostril with your thumb. Open your left nostril to breathe out.

5 Breathe in through your left nostril.

6 Close your left nostril. Open your right nostril. Breathe out through your right nostril.

7 Breathe in through your right nostril. Close it and breathe out through your left one.

8 Begin with three rounds of the breathing exercise and build up to six.

9 When you finish the exercise, release your hands and take a few breaths.

'ANULOM VILOM' MEANS 'ALTERNATE NOSTRIL' IN SANSKRIT.

BUSY BEE BREATH

1 Sit in a comfortable position with your spine straight. Close your eyes. Take a few comfortable breaths.

2 Inhale. Bring your fingers to your ears and close them.

3 As you exhale; make the buzzing sound of a bee.

4 Inhale and repeat.

MINDFULNESS

MINDFULNESS WITH MOKSHA

Hello! My name is Moksha and I am here to
teach you mindfulness. I love mindfulness;
it focuses my mind, helps me concentrate
and makes me feel so calm and happy.
Mindfulness is simply awesome and I am so
happy to share my practice with you.

MOKSHA EXPLAINS MINDFULNESS

Mindfulness is being aware of the present moment. Of taking some time to think about what we are doing rather than just doing it without a single thought. Every thing that we do and every word that we say has some effect somewhere, so before you do anything, you must take a second to think.

Our mind has the tendency to wander off into the past (or the future), never staying in this moment that we're in. Mindfulness will help build your attention, your concentration and clarity of thought, so begin the practice of mindfulness today and strengthen it every day, bit by bit.

The practices here will help build your focus and concentration to help you live in the present moment and enjoy life to its fullest and best.

SITTING MEDITATION

1 Sit in a comfortable position with your spine straight and your eyes closed.

2 Inhale deeply, and as you exhale chant 'Om' (or any other sound that may resonate with you).

3 Breathe and chant a few times. Keeping your eyes closed, focus on the point in-between your eyebrows. Imagine it shining like a diamond.

OMMMM

4 Focus on your breath when you feel your attention wandering.

5 Stay in this state for a few minutes. Slowly open your eyes.

6 Gradually increase the time you spend in this meditative state.

WAYS TO SIT FOR MEDITATION

Experiment with these for more yoga fun.

Sukhasana: Bring one leg over the other to sit in a cross-legged position, keeping your back straight.

Vajrasana: Tuck your heels underneath your hips, keeping your back straight.

Lotus: This can be hard to do at first, but try sitting like this for a few seconds and then slowly increase the time.

CIRCLE OF CONCENTRATION

'DRISHTI' MEANS 'FOCUS' IN SANSKRIT. WHEN YOU ARE MEDITATING, TRY TO FIND YOUR DRISHTI; IT WILL KEEP YOU FOCUSED, CALM AND STEADY.

1 Create a small 'circle of concentration' using a piece of thread or a ribbon. Choose a place (perhaps a room or a garden) where there are minimal distractions.

2 Walk slowly round the 'circle of concentration', focusing your mind on every step you take. If you feel your attention or your mind diverting, step outside the circle.

3 Take a few steps outside the circle and then come back inside when you are ready to focus again.

YOGA NIDRA

'YOGA NIDRA'
MEANS
'YOGA SLEEP'.

1 Lie down in savasana (pg 49). Spend a few moments paying attention to your breath and relaxing your body and mind.

2 You now have to focus on each part of your body, starting with your toes and moving up to your head.

3 Focus on your toes. Scrunch them up. Release.

4 Now tense both your feet. Lift them an inch off the ground. Bring them down. Relax.

5 Focus on the muscles in your calves. Tense them. Relax.

6 Focus on your knees. Relax.

7 Focus on both your legs. Tense them. Lift them an inch off the ground. Relax.

8 Focus on your tummy. Tense all your tummy muscles. Relax.

9 Focus on your back. Feel all your back muscles. Relax.

10 Scrunch your shoulders up to your ears. Tense them. Relax.

11 Make your hands into tight fists. Squeeze all the muscles in your arms. Raise your arms an inch off the ground. Relax.

TENSING MY BODY GETS RID OF THE TENSION IN MY MIND.

12 Close your eyes. Scrunch your nose, forehead and lips, making a small ball of your face. Open your mouth, make a sighing sound. Relax.

13 Take a few seconds to pay attention to every part of your body and relax.

14 Stay in savasana for a few minutes. Relax.

ELEPHANTS SPEND 20 OUT OF 24 HOURS MEDITATING. THAT IS WHY WE ARE SO CALM.

VISUALIZATION

1 Sit in a comfortable position or lie down on your mat.

2 Using verbal instructions, try to verbalize the situation that you are about to face.

3 Let's take the example of an exam. This is a visualization that we can use.

4 Imagine sitting at your desk in the classroom. Take a second to feel the wood of the desk and the paper in front of you. Smell the scents of the classroom, the chalkboard and the books.

5 Now focus your attention on the exam paper in front of you.

6 Don't open it, but look at it. Notice the pens, pencils and rubbers that are lying on the table. See your pencil case on the desk.

USE YOUR IMAGINATION TO MAKE YOUR WISHES COME TRUE!

7 Open your exam paper and feel the joy when you see that you know the answer to every single question on the paper.

8 Now take your pen and start writing. You are able to answer every question correctly!

9 Imagine yourself sitting in your classroom — cool, confident, happy and relaxed, bursting with confidence and joy at being able to successfully tackle the exam paper.

10 Now, imagine a different scenario. That of your answer paper being returned to you, with a 100% at the top. You have aced the paper. You are happy, confident and joyous.

11 You can create different visualization processes for different stress-inducing circumstances to prepare your mind in a positive way.

> TIP: Visualization can be made more fun by adding gentle music to the practice.

Visualization is great during exam time, or before a sports competition, a debate or any other event that is likely to be stressful.

Mindfulness practices can be done in segments of 5 minutes.
These can be included at the end of class or done separately.

5 minutes **You're a Yogi**
10–15 minutes **You're a Super Yogi**

CLASS PLANS

01

20-MINUTE CLASS

2 minutes | Start with savasana (p. 49) to calm the body and the mind.

Sit up and chant Om/spiritual sound, three times.

6 minutes | Do three rounds of Sun Salutation (p. 13).

| 2 minutes | Shoulder Stand (p. 23) |

| 2 minutes | Fish (p. 29) |

| 2 minutes | Bridge (p.27) or Wheel (p. 28) |

| 2 minutes | Tummy Sandwich (p. 33) |

<table>
<tr><td>2 minutes</td><td>Cobra (p34) or Bow (p.36)</td></tr>
</table>

2 minutes | Cobra (p34) or Bow (p.36)

Your choice of standing postures: Warrior/Standing Tummy Sandwich/Dancer/Triangle/Tree (p. 41–48)

2 minutes | Final relaxation: Savasana (p. 49)

Final gratitude prayer

02

40-MINUTE CLASS

2 minutes | Start with savasana (p. 49) to calm the body and the mind.

Sit up and chant Om spiritual sound three times.

6 minutes | Do three rounds of Sun Salutation (p. 13).

| 2 minutes | Your choice of warm-up exercises (p. 17–19) |

| 2 minutes | Shoulder Stand (p. 23) |

| 2 minutes | Plough (p. 25) |

| 2 minutes | Fish (p. 29) |

2 minutes	Bridge (p. 27) or Wheel (p. 28)

2 minutes	Tummy sandwich (p. 32)

2 minutes	Cobra (p. 34) or Bow (p. 36)

1 minute	Your choice of Cat and Cow, Roaring Lion or Camel (p. 37–39)

> TIP: Add in **savasana** at regular intervals depending on the pace and energy of the class.

2 minutes

Lotus (p. 40)

5 minutes

Your choice of two standing postures (p. 41–48): Warrior/Standing Tummy Sandwich/Dancer/ Triangle/Tree

2 minutes

Savasana/Transition (p. 49)

5 minutes | Your choice of Pranayama (breathing exercises) (p. 54–61)

3 minutes | Final relaxation: Savasana (p. 49)

Final gratitude prayer

03

60-MINUTE CLASS

2 minutes | Start with savasana to calm the body and the mind (p. 49).

Sit up and chant Om/spiritual sound three times.

10 minutes | Do five rounds of Sun Salutation (p. 13).

1 minute | Savasana/Transition (p. 49)

5 minutes | Your choice of two warm-up exercises (p. 17–19).

2 minutes | Shoulder Stand (p. 23)

2 minutes | Plough (p. 25)

2 minutes | Fish (p. 29)

2 minutes | Bridge (p. 27) or Wheel (p. 28)

2 minutes | Butterfly (p. 31)

SAVASANA BETWEEN
ASANAS IS ALSO A
GOOD WAY TO GET A
STUDENT'S ATTENTION.

2 minutes | Tummy Sandwich (p. 32)

2 minutes | Cobra (p. 34)

2 minutes | Bow (p. 36)

2 minutes | Your choice of Cat and Cow,
Roaring Lion or Camel (p. 37–39)

2 minutes | Lotus (p. 40)

IF YOU FEEL YOU'RE
GETTING TIRED OR RESTLESS
OR YOU NEED TO CALM DOWN,
ADD IN 10–20 SECONDS OF
SAVASANA BETWEEN THE
ASANAS.

5 minutes	Your choice of two standing postures (p. 41–48): Warrior/Standing Tummy Sandwich/Dancer/ Triangle/Tree

2 minutes	Savasana/Transition (p. 49)
10 minutes	Your choice of two Pranayama (breathing) practices (p. 54–61)

5 minutes	Final relaxation: Savasana (p. 49) Final gratitude prayer

We hope you liked the book.

Till next time!

Om Tat Sat.

SANSKRIT NAMES FOR THE ASANAS

Sun Salutation – Surya Namaskar

Shoulder Stand – Sarvāngāsana

Plough Pose – Halāsana

Bridge Pose – Setubāndhāsana

Wheel Pose – Chakrāsana

Fish Pose – Matsyāsana

Butterfly Pose – Baddhakonāsana

Tummy Sandwich (sitting) Pose
– Paščimottānāsana

Cobra Pose – Bhujašgāsana

Bow Pose – Dhanurāsana

Cat – Cow Pose – Mārjāryāsana
(Cat Pose) and Bitilāsana (Cow Pose)

Roaring Lion Pose – Simhāsana

Camel Pose – Uttrāsana

Lotus Pose – Padmāsana

Warrior Pose – Virābhadrāsana

Standing Tummy Sandwich Pose
– Padhāstaāsana

Dancer Pose – Natarājāsana

Triangle Pose – Trikonāsana

Tree Pose – Vrkshāsana

Corpse Pose – Šavāsana

ACKNOWLEDGEMENTS

I AM EVER
GRATEFUL

The *Om the Yoga Dog* series is truly a passion project for me,
and I love this dog with all my heart. But not as much as I love
the inspiration behind the book; my own dog Princhu, and his life
partner Lucy. It is Princhu's perfect downward dogs that gave birth
to *Om the Yoga Dog*. The love of my two doggies and best friends
has lifted me up in the darkest of moments. There is never a day
when they fail to bring a smile to my face. This book is dedicated
to Prichu, Lucy and all the other pets out there who bring a real
brightness and joy to our lives. May Om brighten up your
day as much as Princhu and Lucy brighten up mine.

NAMAMI
YOGA

The Namami Yoga Foundation, founded by Ira Trivedi,
aspires to make yoga accessible to one and all.
Every class you take and every T-shirt you buy
empowers a girl child in India, making it possible
for her to practise and teach yoga.

Visit www.namamiyoga.com